The Wizard of Id Frammin at the Jim Jam Frippin In the Krotz

Brant Parker and Johnny Hart

CORONET BOOKS
Hodder Fawcett, London

Copyright © 1969, 1970 by Field Newspaper Syndicate
Copyright © 1974 by Fawcett Publications, Inc.
First published 1974 by Fawcett Publications Inc.,
New York

Coronet Edition 1977

Printed and bound in Great Britain for
Hodder Fawcett Ltd., Mill Road,
Dunton Green, Sevenoaks, Kent
(Editorial Office: 47 Bedford Square,
London WC1 3DP), by
Hunt Barnard Printing Ltd.,
Aylesbury, Bucks.

ISBN 0 340 21817 7

6-23

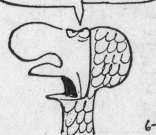

6-26

SIRE!...SOME PEASANT JUST ENTERED A **500** POUND CUCUMBER IN THE COUNTY FAIR!

WHAT DO YOU MAKE OF THAT, WIZ?

7-1.

A 500 POUND PICKLE.

7-2

7-12

WHY IS IT, YOU CAN NEVER FIND A HANDKERCHIEF WHEN YOU **NEED** IT?

7-14

3

8-2

8-4

8-5

8-6

HEAR YE... HEAR YE!...

...ALL PEASANTS WILL GATHER IN THE COURTYARD FOR A GRIEVANCE HEARING!

.WHAT FOR?... IT DIDN'T DO US ANY GOOD LAST YEAR!

8-7

THE KING SAYS "THIS YEAR WILL BE DIFFERENT."

...NOW MY 42ND GRIEVANCE CONCERNS YOUR ATTITUDE...

8-13

THE ENEMY HAS A NEW SECRET WEAPON!

WHAT **IS** IT?

THE WOMEN'S GARDEN CLUB... I WAS PRUNED, SPLICED AND TRANSPLANTED THREE TIMES.

4

THERE'S WORD OF AN ITALIAN PAINTER WHO IS ACCLAIMED THE WORLD OVER...

...HE DOES CEILING MURALS WHILE LYING ON HIS BACK!

8-18

THERE; BUT FOR A LITTLE TALENT AND AN 80 FOOT BRUSH....

8-19

8-28

9-2

9-3

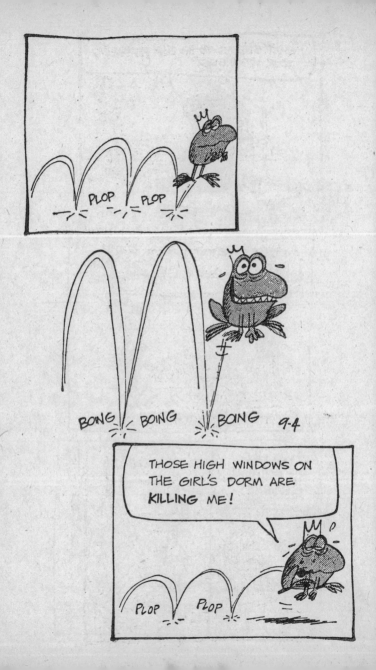

9-5

5

9-20

9-22

9.26

BENNY THE TORCH, COMING UP FOR PAROLE, SIRE!

WELL, BENNY, HAS SIX YEARS IN MY DUNGEON TAUGHT YOU ANYTHING?

I'M CHANGING MY WAYS, KING.

HMMMM,... MAYBE HE HAS LEARNED HIS LESSON

HAVE YOU LINED UP A JOB YET?

NO... I'VE LEARNED MY LESSON.

9·29

10-7

10·11

10-16

10-20

6

10-21

10-23

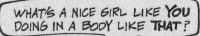

10-27

7

11-14

11-25

12-9

12-16

12·17

8

12-23

12-30

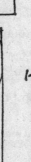

1-21

WIZARD OF ID BOOKS AVAILABLE IN CORONET

JOHNNY HART AND BRANT PARKER

All these books are available at your local bookshop or newsagent, or can be ordered direct from the publisher. Just tick the titles you want and fill in the form below.

Prices and availability subject to change without notice.

CORONET BOOKS, P.O. Box 11, Falmouth, Cornwall.

Please send cheque or postal order, and allow the following for postage and packing:

U.K. – One book 19p plus 9p per copy for each additional book ordered up to a maximum of 73p.

B.F.P.O. and EIRE – 19p for the first book plus 9p per copy for the next 6 books, thereafter 3p per book.

OTHER OVERSEAS CUSTOMERS – 20p for the first book and 10p per copy for each additional book.

Name ....

Address ....

....